MEDICARE INSURANCE

Simplified

(2021)

BY LINDA A. BELL

Medicare Insurance *Simplified* (2021)
Linda A. Bell

Copyright © 2021 Linda A. Bell

ISBN-13: 9798584840167

Printed in the United States of America

Medical / Medicaid & Medicare / 2021 Medicare insurance / Linda A. Bell - first edition

PREFACE

Every day for the next decade, about 10,000 people in the USA will turn 65 and become eligible for Medicare benefits. Imagine that! For many of them, this will be the best and most affordable health insurance coverage they've ever had. For others... not so much. If you don't enroll at the right time and choose the right plan, you may have some large gaps in your coverage and a lot of out-of-pocket costs. But figuring out your Medicare options can be a daunting task!

This book will give you a simple, yet comprehensive overview of how Medicare works.

You will learn:
- What Original Medicare Part A & Part B (the insurance you get from the federal government) covers, doesn't cover, and costs.
- How Part C, Part D, and Medigap plans help you fill the gaps in coverage and minimize your financial risk.
- When you can enroll in or make a change to your plan.

Having this knowledge will empower you with the ability to make an informed decision about the type of Medicare coverage you'd like to have.

CONTENTS

MEDICARE IN A NUTSHELL

Let's begin with a quick overview of some Medicare basics.

Original Medicare has just two parts: Part A & Part B

Part A: hospital/inpatient insurance
- **This covers** your inpatient hospital stay, skilled nursing care in a skilled nursing facility, home health care, and hospice care services.
- **Your cost** includes a monthly premium, hospital deductible, hospital coinsurance, and skilled nursing facility coinsurance.

Part B: medical/outpatient insurance
- **This covers** your medically necessary services, mental health care, preventative and screening services, and durable medical equipment.
- **Your cost** includes a monthly premium, annual deductible, medical copayment, and medical coinsurance.

This federal health insurance program is for people 65 years of age and older, people under 65 with a qualifying disability, and people of any age with End-Stage Renal Disease (ESRD) or Amyotrophic Lateral Sclerosis, also known as Lou Gehrig's Disease (ALS).

NOTE: There is NO LIMIT on Part A & Part B out-of-pocket costs for those who are enrolled in Original Medicare alone.

Don't panic! You have more options.

Medicare Advantage plans (Part C), Medicare Prescription Drug plans (Part D), and Medigap plans (a-n) are available through private companies that have been approved by Medicare.

Medicare Advantage plans (Part C)

- **These plans cover** all of your Part A & Part B benefits and (usually) prescription drug coverage, plus extras. There are six types of Medicare Advantage plans: HMO, HMO-POS, MSA, PFFS, PPO, and SNP. Most of these plans have a provider network.
- **Your cost** includes a monthly premium, annual deductible, copayment, and coinsurance.

Medicare Prescription Drug coverage (Part D)

- **These plans cover** prescription drugs.
- **Your cost** includes a monthly premium, annual deductible, copayment, and coinsurance.

Medicare Supplement Insurance (Medigap plans a, b, c, d, f, g, k, l, m, n)

- **These plans cover** some of your Part A & Part B out-of-pocket costs. Some Medigap plans also cover services that Original Medicare doesn't cover, such as foreign travel emergency care.
- **Your cost** includes a monthly premium.

"Why would anyone want to get their Medicare benefits from a private insurance company instead of the federal government?"

Original Medicare insurance is very good, but it doesn't cover everything and there are many gaps in coverage. The out-of-pocket costs associated with Part A & Part B can add up to a substantial amount of money!

Medicare Advantage plans, Medicare Prescription Drug plans, and Medigap plans can help you fill some of the gaps in Original Medicare coverage, and minimize your financial risk.

Let's take a closer look at all of your Medicare options.

MEDICARE PART

A

ORIGINAL MEDICARE

HOSPITAL [INPATIENT] INSURANCE

PART A COVERS
INPATIENT HOSPITAL CARE

Part A covers your inpatient hospital care when a doctor formally admits you to a hospital that accepts Medicare to treat your illness or injury if all required conditions are met. This includes inpatient care in:

- **Acute care hospitals**
- **Critical access hospitals** (small hospitals in rural areas)
- **Long-term-care hospitals** that specialize in treating patients who are hospitalized for more than 25 days, such as those who use a ventilator for an extended period of time, have experienced a severe wound or head injury, or have an ongoing medical condition that may not improve and treatment is medically necessary to help prevent it from getting worse.
- **Psychiatric hospitals/psychiatric hospital units**
- **Rehabilitation facilities** (inpatient)
- **Religious non-medical health care institutions** when your religious beliefs do not allow you to receive medical care. Medicare will cover the non-religious, non-medical items and services provided in a RNHCI, such as your room, meals, and unmedicated wound dressings.

Inpatient hospital care includes (but may not be limited to): drugs as part of your inpatient treatment (including methadone to treat an opioid use disorder) • general nursing • meals • other hospital services and supplies • semi-private rooms

PART A COVERS
SKILLED NURSING CARE IN A SKILLED NURSING FACILITY

Part A covers skilled care in a skilled nursing facility (SNF) on a short-term basis if all required conditions are met.
- You must have Part A, with days left in your benefit period.
- You are entering the SNF within 30-days of leaving a hospital where you had a 3-day qualifying hospital stay.
- Your doctor has decided that you need daily skilled care that must be given by, or under the supervision of, skilled nursing or therapy staff in a SNF that's certified by Medicare.
- You need skilled services for a medical condition that's either a hospital-related medical condition treated during your hospital stay or a condition that started while you were getting care in the SNF for a hospital-related medical condition.

NOTE: During the COVID-19 pandemic, some exceptions may be made to the criteria for coverage.

Skilled nursing care in a skilled nursing facility includes (but may not be limited to): ambulance transportation to the nearest supplier of needed services that aren't available at the SNF when other transportation endangers health • dietary counseling • meals • medical social services • medications • medical supplies and equipment • occupational therapy • physical therapy • semi-private room • skilled nursing care • speech-language pathology services

PART A COVERS

HOME HEALTH CARE

Part A covers eligible home health care services if all required conditions are met. A doctor, or a health care professional who works with your doctor, must see you face-to-face and certify that you need home health services because you have trouble leaving your home without help due to an illness or injury, and recommend that you not leave home because of your condition. (You may be able to leave home for medical treatments or short, infrequent absences for non-medical reasons, such as to attend religious services.)

Home health care includes (but may not be limited to): injectible osteoporosis drugs for women • intermittent skilled nursing care • medical social services • occupational therapy • part-time home health aide services (for personal hands-on care) • physical therapy • speech-language pathology services

PART A COVERS
HOSPICE CARE SERVICES

Part A covers hospice care services to manage symptoms and pain related to a terminal illness if all required conditions are met. A hospice doctor and your doctor must certify that you are terminally ill and have a life expectancy of six months or less.

NOTE: Hospice patients receive palliative care, which is care that's focused on keeping you comfortable, rather than curing your illness.

Hospice care services include (but may not be limited to): dietary counseling • doctor services • durable medical equipment • grief and loss counseling (for you and your family) • hospice aide and homemaker services • medical supplies nursing care • occupational therapy services • physical therapy services • prescription drugs (for pain relief or symptom control) • short-term inpatient care (for pain and symptom management) • short-term respite care • social work services • speech-language pathology services

"Am I an inpatient or an outpatient?"

If a doctor has not formally admitted you to a hospital or other facility, you are an **outpatient.** All of your medical services, X-rays, lab tests, outpatient surgeries, hospital emergency services, and other outpatient services and supplies are covered by Part B, even if you stay overnight in a hospital bed under observation.

If a doctor has formally admitted you to a hospital or other facility, you are an **inpatient.** Your semi-private room, meals, general nursing care, drugs, and other hospital services are covered by Part A, and most of the medical services you receive from doctors in the hospital are covered by Part B.

NOTE: If your doctor transfers you from the hospital to a rehab center instead of discharging you to go home, your inpatient/outpatient status will play an important role in determining how much you will pay for the cost of your care when you get there!

Medicare only covers the cost of skilled nursing care in a skilled nursing facility (SNF) if you meet all of the criteria for coverage, which includes a "qualifying" 3-day minimum inpatient hospital stay. Your hospital admission day counts towards this 3-day rule, but your discharge day doesn't. The time that you spent in the ER, or while under observation prior to your admission, doesn't count either.

So, if you're not sure what your hospital status is, *ask!*

MEDICARE PART

A

HOSPITAL [INPATIENT] INSURANCE

YOUR COST FOR PART A (2021)

MONTHLY PREMIUM

$0/month*

*Part A is premium-free for most people, because you've worked and had Medicare taxes withheld from your paycheck for at least 40 quarters (10 years). You may also qualify for premium-free Part A based on the work history of a spouse or a parent who is eligible for Social Security benefits if:
- You have been married for at least one year.
- You are single, divorced, and you were married for at least ten years.
- You are single, widowed, and you were married for at least nine months before your spouse died.
- You are a disabled adult child and qualify for DAC benefits.

If you're not eligible for premium-free Part A, your monthly premium is based on the number of quarters of Medicare taxes you've paid.

30-39 quarters	**$259**/month
Less than 30 quarters	**$471**/month

Late-enrollment penalty
If you are not eligible for premium-free Part A and you don't enroll in Part A when you're first eligible for coverage, you may pay a 10% higher premium for twice the number of years in which you could've had Part A but didn't.

YOUR COST FOR PART A (2021)

HOSPITAL DEDUCTIBLE

$1,484 (per benefit period)

You must pay this amount when you are formally admitted to the hospital before Medicare Part A will begin to pay its share of the cost for your hospital/inpatient care.

NOTE: A benefit period begins the day you are formally admitted to the hospital by a doctor as an inpatient; it ends when you have received no inpatient care in a hospital or skilled nursing facility for a full 60 days in a row.

There's no limit to the number of benefit periods a person can have in their lifetime. **It's possible to have as many as six benefit periods in one year!**

Potential financial risk:

$1,484 hospital deductible x 6 benefit periods = $8,904

YOUR COST FOR PART A (2021)

HOSPITAL COINSURANCE

Days 1-60 (per benefit period)	$0/day
Days 61-90 (per benefit period)	$371/day

After you've paid the hospital deductible, this is your share of the cost for the first 90-days of your hospital/inpatient care.

Lifetime Reserve Days
Medicare helps you pay for up to 60 more days (following a 90-day hospital stay) per lifetime.

60 Lifetime Reserve days	$742/day
After Lifetime Reserve days	**You pay 100%**

Your last inpatient day is the day *before* you are discharged.

NOTE: There's a 190-day lifetime limit on a psychiatric hospital inpatient stay.

Potential financial risk:

Days 61-90 (30 days) @ $371/day = $11,130

60 Lifetime Reserve days @ $742/day = $44,520

After that, you pay 100%

YOUR COST FOR PART A (2021)

SKILLED NURSING FACILITY COINSURANCE

Days 1-20 (per benefit period)	$0/day
Days 21-100 (per benefit period)	$185.50/day
After that (per benefit period)	You pay 100%

This is your share of the cost for skilled nursing care provided in a skilled nursing facility.

Potential financial risk:

Days 21-100 (80 days) @ $185.50/day = $14,840

After 100 days you pay 100%

MEDICARE PART

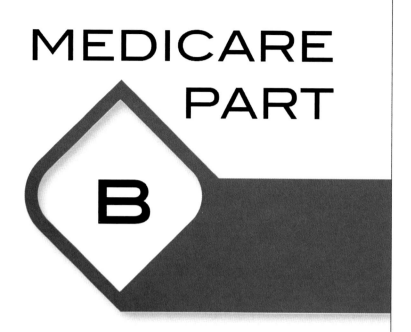

B

ORIGINAL
MEDICARE

MEDICAL [OUTPATIENT] INSURANCE

PART B COVERS
MEDICALLY NECESSARY SERVICES

Part B covers medically necessary services or supplies that are needed to diagnose or treat your medical condition, and that meet "accepted standards of medical practice." This includes visits to doctors, specialists, and other health care providers who accept Medicare assignment. (See "Part B Medical Coinsurance" to learn more about Medicare assignment.)

Medically necessary services include (but may not be limited to): acupuncture (up to 12 visits in 90 days for chronic low back pain; 8 additional visits if you show improvement; 20 visits maximum per year) · ambulance services · chemotherapy · chiropractic services (limited) · clinical research studies · clinical lab services · diabetes self-management training · diagnostic tests · doctor and other health care provider services, including those received in the hospital when you are an inpatient · outpatient hospital services · second surgical opinion · telehealth (covers certain medical or health services, such as office visits, psychotherapy, and consultations)

PART B COVERS
MENTAL HEALTH CARE

Part B covers mental health care services including visits to doctors, specialists, and other health care providers who accept Medicare assignment. It also covers medically necessary services and supplies to diagnose or treat your mental health condition.

Mental health care includes (but may not be limited to): certain prescription drugs (those that aren't usually self-administered, like some injections) • depression screening (one per year) • diagnostic tests • family counseling, if the main purpose is to help with your treatment • individual and group psychotherapy • medication management • partial hospitalization • psychiatric evaluation • testing to find out if you're getting the services you need and if your current treatment is helping you • "Welcome to Medicare" one-time preventive visit • yearly "Wellness" visit

PART B COVERS
PREVENTIVE AND SCREENING SERVICES

Part B covers preventive and screening services to prevent illness or detect it at an early stage. If you receive these services from a health care provider who accepts Medicare assignment, you pay nothing for most of these services.

Preventive and screening services include (but may not be limited to): abdominal aortic aneurysm screening • alcohol misuse screenings and counseling • bone mass measurements (bone density) • cardiovascular disease screenings • cardiovascular disease (behavioral therapy) • cervical and vaginal cancer screening • colorectal cancer screenings (multi-target stool DNA tests, screening barium enemas, screening colonoscopies, screening fecal occult blood test, screening flexible sigmoidoscopies) • depression screenings • diabetes screenings • diabetes self-management training • flu shots • glaucoma tests • hepatitis B shots • hepatitis B Virus (HBV) infection screening • hepatitis C screening test • HIV screening • lung cancer screening • mammograms (screening) • nutrition therapy services • obesity screenings and counseling • one-time "Welcome to Medicare" preventive visit • pneumococcal shots • prostate cancer screenings • sexually transmitted infections screening and counseling • tobacco use cessation counseling • yearly "Wellness" visit

PART B COVERS
DURABLE MEDICAL EQUIPMENT

Medicare Part B covers medically necessary durable medical equipment prescribed by a doctor for home care.

Durable medical equipment includes (but may not be limited to): blood sugar monitors · blood sugar test strips · canes · commode chairs · continuous passive motion devices · continuous Positive Airway Pressure (CPAP) devices · crutches · hospital beds · infusion pumps and supplies · lancet devices and lancets · nebulizers and nebulizer medications · oxygen equipment and accessories · patient lifts · pressure-reducing support surfaces · suction pumps · traction equipment · walkers · wheelchairs and scooters

Original Medicare does NOT cover:

> Cosmetic surgery
> Hearing exams for hearing aids
> Medical care while traveling outside the USA (with rare exceptions)
> Outpatient prescription drugs
> Routine dental services or dentures
> Routine eye exams for glasses
> Routine foot care
> Routine preventative physical exams

YOUR COST

MEDICARE PART

B

MEDICAL [OUTPATIENT] INSURANCE

YOUR COST FOR PART B (2021)

MONTHLY PREMIUM

$148.50/month*

If you receive Social Security or Railroad Retirement Board (RRB) benefits, your Medicare Part B monthly premium will be deducted from your benefit check.

If you *don't* receive Social Security or Railroad Retirement Board (RRB) benefits, you'll get a Medicare Premium Bill (Form CMS-500) every three months. You can mail your payment to Medicare, pay it online through your Medicare account, pay it through your bank's online payment system, or use "Medicare Easy Pay" to have the premium automatically deducted from your bank account every month.

*An Income Related Monthly Adjustment Amount (IRMAA) will be added to your Part B monthly premium if the modified adjusted gross income amount that you reported on your income tax return two years ago (in 2019) was more than $88,000 for an individual or $176,000 for a joint return.

Late-enrollment penalty: If you don't enroll in Medicare Part B when you're first eligible for coverage, your monthly premium may go up 10% (of the standard premium amount) for each 12-month period in which you could've had Part B but didn't. This is a lifelong late enrollment penalty.

YOUR COST FOR PART B (2021)

ANNUAL DEDUCTIBLE

$203/year

Every year, you must pay this amount for covered medical/outpatient services before your Medicare Part B will begin to pay.

The annual deductible does not apply to certain preventive services.

YOUR COST FOR PART B (2021)

MEDICAL COPAYMENT

Cost varies

After your deductible is met, you'll usually pay the hospital a copayment (which is typically a fixed dollar amount) for each service you receive in a hospital outpatient setting. This is in addition to the Part B coinsurance that you pay for most doctor services.

Certain preventive services have no copay.

NOTE: **Doctors may charge more for outpatient services that are provided in a hospital if the same services can be provided in their office. Your copay *for each service* will generally be capped at the Part A hospital deductible, $1,484.** (If the services are provided in a critical access hospital, your copay may be higher.)

There's NO ANNUAL LIMIT on your Part B out-of-pocket costs if you have Original Medicare alone!

YOUR COST FOR PART B (2021)

MEDICAL COINSURANCE

Typically 20%*

After your deductible is met, this is the amount you'll typically pay for most Medicare-approved doctor services (including most services you get from doctors in the hospital when you are an inpatient), durable medical equipment, outpatient therapy, and Part B drugs, such as chemotherapy.

Doctors, providers, and suppliers who **accept Medicare assignment** are those who have agreed to be paid directly by Medicare, and will accept the Medicare-approved amount as full payment for covered services.

Non-participating providers are those who have not agreed to accept Medicare assignment. If they choose to accept assignment for individual services, they **may charge an EXCESS CHARGE of up to 15% over and above the Medicare-approved amount** (if their state allows it).

Doctors and other providers may also **opt-out** of working with Medicare (other than providing emergency or urgently needed medical care) for two years at a time. During this period, they will not be paid by Medicare for any services or covered items you receive from them. If you want to see a provider who has opted-out, you and the provider can set up payment terms that you both agree on.

PART A & PART B ENROLLMENT PERIODS

You can only enroll in or make a change to your Medicare coverage during specific enrollment periods.

Initial Enrollment Period (IEP)

You have a 7-month window of time to enroll in Medicare Part A & Part B for the first time. It begins three months before the month you turn 65, includes the month you turn 65, and ends three months after the month you turn 65. *(If your birthday is on the 1st day of the month, your coverage starts the first day of the prior month.)*

Let's say your 65th birthday is APR 20. You will have from JAN 1 - JUL 31 to enroll in Medicare for the first time. The best time to enroll is during the three months before your birthday so your coverage can go into effect on APR 1. If you wait, your coverage will be delayed.

Using this example, if you enroll in Medicare:
- JAN - MAR: Your coverage starts on APR 1.
- APR: Your coverage starts (in **one month**) on MAY 1
- MAY: Your coverage starts (in **two months**) on JUL 1.
- JUN: Your coverage starts (in **three months**) on SEP 1.
- JUL: Your coverage starts (in **three months**) on OCT 1.

If you are receiving Social Security benefits, you will automatically be enrolled in Original Medicare. Your (red, white, and blue) Medicare ID card will arrive in the mail about three months before your 65th birthday. Your Medicare Part A & Part B effective dates will be printed on your card. (If you live in Puerto Rico you must sign up for Part B; you won't get it automatically.)

If you are NOT receiving Social Security benefits, contact Social Security three months before you turn 65 to enroll in Medicare. If you're eligible for premium-free Part A you can enroll anytime after you're eligible with no late enrollment penalty, because you've already paid for Part A with taxes. Your coverage retroactively starts six months before you signed up, but no earlier than your first month of eligibility.

If you are under 65 and receiving Social Security Disability benefits, you will automatically be enrolled in Part A & Part B after you have received Social Security benefits (or certain Railroad Retirement Board disability benefits) for 24 months.

If you are any age with ALS (Lou Gehrig's Disease) your Medicare coverage will start immediately upon collecting Social Security Disability benefits.

If you are any age with ESRD (End-Stage Renal Disease) you'll need to sign up for Medicare. Your coverage will generally start three months after a course of regular dialysis begins, or after a kidney transplant.

"Should I delay my Part B enrollment?"

If you or your spouse are still *actively* working when you

turn 65, or if you have other insurance coverage, contact your benefits administrator to find out how your insurance works with Medicare. In some cases, you may need to enroll in Part A & Part B to keep your coverage. In other cases, it may be better to delay your Part B enrollment.

If you (or your spouse) work for a company with 20 OR MORE EMPLOYEES, your group health plan is your primary insurer and Medicare is secondary. You should enroll in Medicare Part A during your Initial Enrollment Period if you qualify for premium-free Part A, as this may save you money if you are hospitalized. But as a general rule, you should delay your Part B enrollment until you (or your spouse) stop working or you lose your employer coverage, whichever comes first. This will save you from paying a monthly premium for a secondary insurance plan. More importantly, it will preserve your 6-month Medigap Open Enrollment Period, which is triggered automatically when a person who is 65 or older enrolls in Part B. If you have any serious pre-existing health conditions and want to have Medigap coverage after you retire, it's vital to delay this enrollment period because during this time you are *guaranteed* to be covered, and at the same rate as a healthy person. After this once-in-a-lifetime enrollment period has passed, you may be required to go through medical underwriting to determine your insurability. You could be declined, have a waiting period, and/or pay a higher premium than other people (unless you qualify for a Special Enrollment Period or your state doesn't allow medical underwriting of Medigap plans).

NOTE: Contact the Social Security Administration or Medicare *before* your Part B coverage begins to let them know you are still actively working. Ask them how the Part B coverage pertains to your specific employment situation.

If you (or your spouse) work for a company with LESS THAN 20 EMPLOYEES, you need to enroll in Medicare Part A & Part B during your Initial Enrollment Period (unless your employer is part of a multiple or multi-employer group in which at least one employer employs 20 or more individuals), even if you have a group health plan. According to the Medicare Secondary Payer Act, in this situation, Medicare will be your primary insurer and your group health plan will be secondary. If you don't enroll in Medicare Part A & Part B when you turn 65, your group health plan may not pay on any claims because there is no primary insurer to process the claim first.

General Enrollment Period (GEP) JAN 1 - MAR 31

If you did not enroll in Medicare Part A and/or Part B when you were first eligible, and you are not eligible for a Special Enrollment Period (SEP), you may enroll during this election period. Coverage starts JULY 1. A lifelong late enrollment penalty may apply.

Special Circumstances | Special Enrollment Periods (SEP)

When certain life events happen after your Initial Enrollment Period has passed, you may be able to use a Special Enrollment Period to enroll in Medicare Part A and/or Part B. For example, if you or your spouse are currently working, and you are covered by a group health plan through the employer or union, you have an **8-month Special Enrollment Period** to enroll in Part A and/or Part B. Your SEP starts on the month after the employment ends, or the month after the group health insurance plan (that's based on the current employment) ends; whichever happens *first*.

If you have a disability and your group health plan coverage is based on the current employment of a family member, the employer must have 100 or more employees for you to qualify for a Special Enrollment Period.

When you're ready to enroll in Part B: You will need to fill out two Social Security forms: CMS-40B and CMS-L564. (Your employer will need to complete a section on the CMS-L564 form to verify that you had group healthcare coverage.) Make a copy of the signed and completed forms for your records before you send them to your local Social Security office. You can also submit them online.

Retiree coverage, VA coverage, COBRA, and individual health insurance plans purchased through a health insurance marketplace do NOT meet the definition of "coverage based on current employment."

MEDICARE PART C

AVAILABLE THROUGH PRIVATE COMPANIES

MEDICARE ADVANTAGE PLAN

PART C: MEDICARE ADVANTAGE PLAN

Medicare Advantage plans (Part C) are often referred to as bundled or all-in-one plans. They provide an alternative way to receive your Medicare Part A & Part B benefits. You still have Medicare but get most of your Part A & Part B benefits from a private insurance company instead of the federal government, which pays these plans to manage your care and cover almost all of your medically necessary services. (Original Medicare covers the cost of hospice care services, some of the costs for clinical research studies, and some new Medicare benefits.)

Most Medicare Advantage plans have a network of providers. Some will allow you to go out-of-network for a higher cost. All plans cover you for emergency and urgently needed medical care everywhere in the U.S. and its territories. And as of JAN 1, 2021, all Medicare Advantage plans must cover people who have ESRD (End-Stage Renal Disease).

NOTE: A Medicare Advantage plan is NOT a Medicare Supplement.

To be eligible for Part C you must have Part A & Part B, live in the plan's service area, and can't be incarcerated. If you have an employer, union, or retiree insurance plan, enrolling in a Medicare Advantage plan could cause you and your dependents to lose your coverage and you may not be able to get it back. Call your benefits provider before you enroll in a plan.

There are six types of Medicare Advantage plans:

Health Maintenance Organization (HMO)

In most HMO plans, you can only go to doctors, other health care providers, or hospitals that are in the plan's network. You may need a referral from your primary care doctor to visit other doctors and specialists, or to have medically necessary tests.

HMO Point-Of-Service (HMO-POS)

This type of HMO plan allows you to get some services out-of-network, generally at a higher cost.

Medical Savings Account (MSA)

A Medicare MSA plan combines a high deductible Medicare Advantage plan with a savings account that Medicare contributes to. (The maximum deductible in 2021 is $14,500.) After you've met the deductible, the plan pays for 100% of your Medicare-covered services for the rest of the year. MSA's don't include prescription drug coverage; you can add Part D.

Preferred Provider Organization (PPO)

You can go to doctors, hospitals, and other Medicare providers outside the plan's network, generally at a higher cost.

Private Fee-For-Service (PFFS)

Each plan specifies how much the doctors, other health care providers, and hospitals will get paid, and what you must pay for out-of-pocket. You can generally go to any Medicare-approved provider who accepts the plan's payment terms. If the plan doesn't include drug coverage, you can add Part D.

Special Needs Plan (SNP)

Enrollment is limited to those who meet specified eligibility criteria. There are three types of SNP plans: Chronic condition (C-SNP), Dual eligible (D-SNP), and Institutional (I-SNP).

PART C

INCLUDES YOUR PART A BENEFITS

Part A covers:

INPATIENT HOSPITAL CARE

SKILLED NURSING CARE IN A SKILLED NURSING FACILITY

HOME HEALTH CARE

HOSPICE CARE SERVICES

PART C
INCLUDES YOUR PART B BENEFITS

Part B covers:

MEDICALLY NECESSARY SERVICES

MENTAL HEALTH CARE

PREVENTIVE AND SCREENING SERVICES

DURABLE MEDICAL EQUIPMENT

PART C

USUALLY INCLUDES PART D

Standard Part D drug plan stages:

STAGE 1:
ANNUAL DEDUCTIBLE

STAGE 2:
INITIAL COVERAGE

STAGE 3:
COVERAGE GAP

STAGE 4:
CATASTROPHIC COVERAGE

PART C

USUALLY INCLUDES EXTRA BENEFITS

Such as:

ROUTINE DENTAL CARE

ROUTINE EYE CARE

ROUTINE HEARING CARE

OTHER HEALTH AND WELLNESS PROGRAMS

Annual Notice of Changes (ANOC) | Evidence of Coverage (EOC)

In the fall, your Medicare Advantage plan will send you a printed **Annual Notice of Changes (ANOC)** about upcoming changes to your plan's coverage, costs, service area, and more that will go into effect on JAN 1. You will also receive a notice (or printed copy) of the **Evidence of Coverage (EOC)** about changes in coverage, costs, provider networks, service area, and more. Review both documents carefully. If you're unhappy with the changes, you can switch to another plan during the Annual Enrollment Period (OCT 15 - DEC 7).

Star ratings

Medicare uses a star rating to measure the quality and performance of Medicare Advantage plans. The overall rating tells you about the plan's quality in five areas:
1. Staying healthy (screening tests and vaccines)
2. Managing chronic (long-term) conditions
3. Member experience with the health plan
4. Member complaints and changes in the plan's performance
5. Health plan customer service

This information is collected from:
- Member surveys
- Information that clinicians submit to Medicare
- Information that plans submit to Medicare
- Medicare's regular monitoring activities

If the plan covers prescription drugs, the overall rating tells you about the drug plan's quality and performance as well.

YOUR COST

MEDICARE PART C

MEDICARE ADVANTAGE PLAN

YOUR COST FOR PART C (2021)

MONTHLY PREMIUM

Cost varies (by company and plan)

Each plan sets the price for their monthly premium. Some plans even have a $0/month premium!

If your Medicare Advantage plan has a monthly premium, you can pay it by check, credit card, or automatic debit from a bank account. You can also ask the plan to deduct it from your Social Security or Railroad Retirement Board (RRB) benefits.

If you enroll in a Medicare Advantage plan with a $0/month premium, don't forget to keep paying your Part B monthly premium!

Because you can't have a Medicare Advantage plan (Part C) unless you have Part A and Part B!

YOUR COST FOR PART C (2021)

ANNUAL DEDUCTIBLE

Cost varies (by company and plan)

If your Medicare Advantage plan has an annual deductible, you must pay this amount before your plan will begin to pay.

The deductible does not apply to certain preventive services.

YOUR COST FOR PART C (2021)

COPAYMENT AND COINSURANCE

Cost varies (by company and plan)

After your deductible is met, this is the amount you pay for services and benefits that are included in your plan.

The copayment and coinsurance do not apply to certain preventive services.

YOUR COST FOR PART C (2021)

MAXIMUM OUT-OF-POCKET LIMIT

MOOP varies (by company and plan)

All Medicare Advantage plans have a maximum out-of-pocket (MOOP) limit. This amount is the most you will pay out-of-pocket per year for Medicare-covered services.

PART C
ENROLLMENT PERIODS

You can only enroll in or make a change to a Medicare Advantage plan (Part C) during specific enrollment periods.

Initial Coverage Election Period (ICEP)

If your Part A & Part B have the same effective date you can enroll in a Medicare Advantage plan during your 7-month Initial Enrollment Period (IEP).

If your Part A & Part B have different effective dates because you enrolled in one or the other during a Special Enrollment Period or during the General Enrollment Period, your Part C Initial Coverage Election Period (ICEP) begins three months before the effective date of whichever "part" you added last; it's usually Part B. You have until the last day of the month before your coverage starts to enroll in a Medicare Advantage plan. They will start at the same time.

If you're newly eligible for Medicare because you have a disability and you're under 65 you may enroll in a Medicare Advantage plan after you've received Social Security or Railroad Retirement Board (RRB) disability benefits for a full 24 months. You have seven months to enroll in a plan. (Starts three months before your 25th month, includes the 25th month, and ends three months after your 25th month.) If you enroll during the three months before your 25th month, your coverage starts on the first day of the 25th month. If you enroll in the 25th - 28th month, your coverage starts on the first day of the month after you enroll.

If you're already eligible for Medicare because you have a disability and you turn 65, you may use your (7-month) Initial Enrollment Period (IEP) to:
- Enroll in a Medicare Advantage plan
- Switch to another Medicare Advantage plan
- Disenroll from a Medicare Advantage plan and return to Original Medicare; you may add Part D

12-month Medicare Advantage Trial Period: If you enroll in a Medicare Advantage plan when you are first eligible for coverage at age 65, you can drop your plan and return to Original Medicare at any time before the one-year anniversary of the effective date. You may add Part D to your coverage. You retain your Medigap Guaranteed Issue Rights during this trial period.

Annual Enrollment Period (AEP) OCT 15 - DEC 7

During this enrollment period, you may:
- Enroll in a Medicare Advantage plan
- Switch from one Medicare Advantage plan to another Medicare Advantage plan
- Disenroll from a Medicare Advantage plan and return to Original Medicare; you may add Part D

Changes go into effect on JAN 1.

Medicare Advantage Open Enrollment Period (MA-OEP): JAN 1 - MAR 31

During this time you can make a one-time change:
- Switch from one Medicare Advantage plan to another Medicare Advantage plan
- Disenroll from a Medicare Advantage plan and return to Original Medicare; you may add Part D

Changes start on the first day of the month after the plan gets your request.

Medicare Advantage Open Enrollment Period - New (MA-OEP New)

New Medicare beneficiaries who enroll in a Medicare Advantage plan during their Initial Enrollment Period are entitled to a **3-month Medicare Advantage Trial Period**. During this time, you can make a one-time change to:

- Switch from one Medicare Advantage plan to another Medicare Advantage plan
- Disenroll from a Medicare Advantage plan and return to Original Medicare; you may add Part D

Special Circumstances | Special Enrollment Periods (SEP)

When certain life events happen after your Initial Coverage Election Period (ICEP) has passed, you may be able to use a Special Enrollment Period to enroll in, switch, or drop a Medicare Advantage plan. For example, you have a **2-month Special Enrollment Period** after leaving coverage from your employer or union to enroll in a Medicare Advantage plan.

5-Star Special Enrollment Period (5-Star SEP): DEC 8 - NOV 30

If a 5-star Medicare Advantage plan, 5-star Cost plan, or a 5-star Medicare Prescription Drug plan is available in your service area, you can use this Special Enrollment Period to make a one-time switch to that plan. (A 5-star rating is considered excellent; these ratings can change every year.)

MEDICARE PART

D

AVAILABLE THROUGH PRIVATE COMPANIES

PRESCRIPTION DRUG COVERAGE

PART D: PRESCRIPTION DRUG COVERAGE

Original Medicare does *not* cover outpatient prescription drugs. Medicare Prescription Drug coverage (Part D) is available through private insurance companies as a stand-alone drug plan or as part of a Medicare Advantage plan. Part D covers prescription drugs, biologics (such as allergy shots and gene therapies), insulin (and medical supplies associated with insulin injections), and certain vaccines.

All drug plans must cover at least the standard Part D benefit or its actuarial equivalent. (The value of the coverage must be just as good, or better.)

Each plan decides which prescription drugs they will cover and which pharmacies they will use. You will generally save money by filling your prescriptions at preferred pharmacies if your plan has them. Plans are required to cover both generic and brand-name prescription drugs, with at least two drugs in each therapeutic category. These drugs are generally grouped into cost-sharing tiers, and the plans can choose which tier level each drug goes in.

To be eligible for Medicare Part D, you must be enrolled in Medicare Part A or Part B, live in the plan's service area, and cannot be incarcerated. If you have group health insurance coverage through your employer or union, enrolling in a Part D plan could cause you and your dependents to lose your coverage, and you may not be able to get it back. Call your benefits provider before you enroll in Part D.

Part D Senior Savings Model

Beginning January 2021, drug plans that participate in the Part D Senior Savings Model will offer multiple types of insulin at a $35 maximum copay for a 30-day supply in the Annual Deductible, Initial Coverage, and Coverage Gap stages. People who enroll in a plan that participates in this Model should save an average of $446/year in out-of-pocket costs for their insulin!

Formulary exceptions

If a formulary does not include a specific drug that you take, a similar drug should be available. If you or your doctor believe that none of the drugs on your plan's formulary will work for your condition, you can request a formulary exception. If approved, the plan will cover that particular drug. In most cases, you must first try a certain less-expensive drug on the plan's formulary before you move up to a more expensive drug. This is called step therapy. Your prescriber can request an exception to this rule if you meet certain criteria.

Drugs you get in a hospital outpatient setting

In most cases, self-administered drugs (ones that you would normally take on your own) that are received while you have an outpatient status in a hospital setting, such as when you are under observation in an emergency room, are not covered by Part B. You will likely need to pay out-of-pocket for these. If you submit a claim to your drug plan they *may* cover these drugs and send you a refund.

NOTE: A standard Part D drug plan has four stages of coverage. (Some plans have an alternative benefit structure, which may include some or all of the four stages of coverage.)

PART D

STAGE 1:
ANNUAL DEDUCTIBLE

If your plan has an annual deductible, you must pay this amount (starting at the beginning of each calendar year) before your plan will begin to pay for covered prescription drugs.

If your plan does not have an annual deductible, your coverage begins immediately with Stage 2.

PART D

STAGE 2:
INITIAL COVERAGE

In this stage, you and the drug plan share the cost of covered prescription drugs.

Every time you fill a prescription the plan keeps track of how much you've spent and how much they've spent. If your total drug cost for the year reaches the **Initial Coverage Limit ($4,130)** you'll move into Stage 3.

NOTE: If you receive Extra Help (a low-income subsidy), you will stay in Stage 2 regardless of the amount of your total drug cost. (See: "Part D: Extra Help and SPAP.")

PART D

STAGE 3: COVERAGE GAP

In this stage, you'll pay no more than 25% of the cost for generic drugs and 25% of the undiscounted cost for brand-name drugs. (Some plans provide additional coverage in the Coverage Gap.)

If your true out-of-pocket cost reaches the **Coverage Gap Out-Of-Pocket Threshold ($6,550)** you'll move into Stage 4.

Your true out-of-pocket cost (TrOOP) includes:
- Annual deductible
- Copayments
- Coinsurance
- Manufacturer's discount on brand-name drugs (in the Coverage Gap)
- Amounts paid or borne by the AIDS Drug Assistance Program and the Indian Health Services
- Amounts paid by or through qualified State Pharmaceutical Assistance Program (SPAP), most charities, health savings accounts, flexible spending accounts, and medical savings accounts

Some costs do not apply to the TrOOP, such as:
- Monthly premium
- Pharmacy dispensing fee
- Drugs that are not on your plan's formulary

PART D

STAGE 4:
CATASTROPHIC COVERAGE

In this stage, you will only pay **$3.70** for generic drugs and **$9.20** for brand-name drugs, OR **5%** of the prescription drug cost, *whichever is higher,* for the remainder of the calendar year.

Your monthly drug cost generally goes down in this stage of coverage.

However, if you only paid a $35 copay for insulin medications in Stages 1, 2, and 3 (because your plan participates in the Part D Senior Savings Model) your monthly drug cost may go up in Stage 4.

Annual Notice of Changes (ANOC) | Evidence of Coverage (EOC)

In the fall, your Medicare Prescription Drug plan will send you a printed **Annual Notice of Changes (ANOC)** about upcoming changes to your plan's coverage, costs, service area, and more that will go into effect on JAN 1. You will also receive a notice (or printed copy) of the **Evidence of Coverage (EOC)** about changes in coverage, costs, provider networks, service area, and more. Review both documents carefully. If you're unhappy with the changes, you can switch to another plan during the Annual Enrollment Period (OCT 15 - DEC 7).

Star ratings

Medicare uses a star rating to measure the quality and performance of Medicare Prescription Drug plans. The overall rating tells you about the drug plan's quality and performance in these four areas:

1. Drug plan customer service
2. Member complaints and changes in the drug plan's performance
3. Member experience with the drug plan
4. Drug safety and accuracy of drug pricing

This information is collected from:
- Member surveys
- Billing and other information that plans submit to Medicare
- Medicare's regular monitoring activities

YOUR COST

MEDICARE PART D

PRESCRIPTION DRUG COVERAGE

YOUR COST FOR PART D (2021)

MONTHLY PREMIUM

> **Cost varies** (by company and plan)*

Each plan sets the price for their monthly premium. You can pay it by check, credit card, or automatic debit from a bank account. You can also ask the plan to deduct it from your Social Security or Railroad Retirement Board (RRB) benefits.

*An Income Related Monthly Adjustment Amount (IRMAA) will be added to your Part D monthly premium if the modified adjusted gross income amount that you reported on your income tax return two years ago (in 2019) was more than $88,000 for an individual or $176,000 for a joint return.

Late-enrollment penalty: If you go 63 or more continuous days without having Medicare Part D or other "creditable" coverage after the last day of your Initial Enrollment Period, you may pay a penalty of 1% of the National Base Beneficiary Premium ($32.74 in 2021) times the number of full uncovered months rounded to the nearest $.10, for as long as you have Part D.

"Creditable" coverage means that the coverage is expected to pay on average as much as the standard Medicare Prescription Drug (Part D) coverage.

YOUR COST FOR PART D (2021)

ANNUAL DEDUCTIBLE

Cost varies (by company and plan)
$0 - $445/year

If your drug plan has an annual deductible, you must pay this amount before the plan will pay its share for your covered prescription drugs.

When shopping for a drug plan, look closely at the annual deductible. Some plans apply it to ALL tier levels. Others only apply it to Tier 3, Tier 4, and Tier 5 drugs, which can save you a LOT of money if most of your drugs are Tier 1 and Tier 2!

Some plans have no annual deductible. But, watch out! The monthly premium and drug costs may be higher.

YOUR COST FOR PART D (2021)

COPAYMENT AND COINSURANCE

Cost varies (by company and plan)

Each plan decides which prescription drugs they will cover and how much they will charge. Some drug tier levels have a copayment (dollar amount); others have a coinsurance (percentage of the negotiated cost for that drug).

Before you enroll in a drug plan, check the formulary carefully!

On some plans, all of your drugs may be in Tier 1 and Tier 2; on other plans, they may be in Tier 1 and Tier 3. And some medications may not be covered at all!

YOUR COST FOR PART D (2021)

EXTRA HELP AND SPAP

Medicare **Extra Help** is available for Medicare beneficiaries who need help paying for their prescription drugs.

You may qualify for this low-income subsidy (LIS) if:
- You have Medicare Part A and/or Part B
- You have limited resources
- You live in one of the 50 states or the District of Columbia

You will automatically qualify if:
- You have full Medicaid
- You get SSI (Supplemental Security Income) benefits
- Medicaid helps pay for your Part B premiums (through a Medicare Savings Program)

Those with Extra Help can switch to a different drug plan (or Medicare Advantage plan with prescription drug coverage) one time during each of these three periods: JAN-FEB-MAR, APR-MAY-JUN, JUL-AUG-SEPT. The change is effective on the first day of the following month. (You can also switch during the Annual Enrollment Period from OCT 15 - DEC 7. The change is effective JAN 1.)

If you don't qualify for Extra Help, you may qualify for a **State Pharmaceutical Assistance Program (SPAP)**, such as Senior Rx/Disability Rx.

PART D
ENROLLMENT PERIODS

You can only enroll in or make a change to a Medicare Prescription Drug plan during specific enrollment periods.

Part D Initial Enrollment Period (IEP)

If you have Medicare Part A *or* Part B, you can enroll in a Medicare Prescription Drug plan during your 7-month Initial Enrollment Period (IEP).

If you don't have Part A and you enroll in Part B for the first time during the General Enrollment Period (GEP) between JAN 1 - MAR 31, you can enroll in a drug plan between APR 1 - JUN 30. Coverage starts JULY 1.

If you're newly eligible for Medicare because you have a disability and you are under 65, you may enroll in a Medicare Prescription Drug plan after you've received Social Security or Railroad Retirement Board (RRB) disability benefits for a full 24 months. You have seven months to enroll in a plan. (Starts three months before your 25th month, includes the 25th month, and ends three months after your 25th month.) If you enroll during the three months before your 25th month, your coverage starts on the first day of the 25th month. If you enroll in the 25th - 28th month, your coverage begins on the first day of the month after you enroll.

If you're already eligible for Medicare because you have a disability and you are turning 65, you may use your 7-month Initial Enrollment Period (IEP) to:
- Enroll in Part D

- Switch from one Part D plan to another Part D plan
- Switch from a Part D plan to Medicare Advantage plan with prescription drug coverage

Annual Enrollment Period (AEP) OCT 15 - DEC 7

During this enrollment period, you may:
- Enroll in Part D
- Switch from one Part D plan to another Part D plan
- Switch from a Part D plan to Medicare Advantage plan with prescription drug coverage

Changes go into effect on JAN 1.

Medicare Advantage Open Enrollment Period (MA-OEP): JAN 1 - MAR 31

You may only use this enrollment period to enroll in Part D *if* you've dropped a Medicare Advantage plan and returned to Original Medicare during this MA-OEP. Changes start on the first day of the month after the plan gets your request.

Medicare Advantage Open Enrollment Period-New (MA-OEP New)

You may only use this enrollment period to enroll in Part D if:
- You joined a Medicare Advantage plan during your Initial Enrollment Period
- You qualified for a "3-Month Medicare Advantage Trial Period"
- You are within the 3-month trial period
- You are using this enrollment period to drop your Medicare Advantage plan and return to Original Medicare

Special Circumstances | Special Enrollment Periods (SEP)

When certain life events happen after your Initial Enrollment Period (IEP) has passed, you may be able to use a Special Enrollment Period to enroll in, switch, or drop your Medicare Prescription Drug plan.

5-Star Special Enrollment Period (5-Star SEP) DEC 8 - NOV 30

If a 5-star Medicare Advantage plan, 5-star Cost plan, or a 5-star Medicare Prescription Drug plan is available in your service area, you can use this Special Enrollment Period to make a one-time switch to that plan. (A 5-star rating is considered excellent. These ratings can change every year.)

MEDIGAP PLAN

a~n

AVAILABLE THROUGH PRIVATE COMPANIES

MEDICARE SUPPLEMENT INSURANCE

MEDIGAP: MEDICARE SUPPLEMENT INSURANCE

Medicare Supplement Insurance, called Medigap, is available from private companies to *supplement* Original Medicare. These plans help you pay for some of the costs that Original Medicare does not pay for, such as your copays, coinsurance, etc. Some plans also cover additional services that are not covered by Original Medicare, such as foreign travel emergency care.

All Medigap plans must be clearly identified as "Medicare Supplement Insurance" and must follow federal and state laws that are in place to protect you. These plans are available in all states and Washington D.C.

To be eligible for Medigap, you must be enrolled in Part A & Part B. If you do not enroll during your 6-month Medigap Open Enrollment Period, you may be required to go through medical underwriting, which means that the insurer may take a close look at your medical history, pre-existing conditions, and other risk factors when reviewing your application. As a result of this, you could be denied coverage or have a waiting period. Some states allow special exceptions and/or have additional rules. (See "Medigap Enrollment Periods.")

Each company decides which Medigap plans it wants to sell. They are generally distinguished by their plan letter, such as Medigap Plan a, Plan b, Plan c, Plan d, Plan f, Plan g, Plan k, Plan l, Plan m, and Plan n. Companies are not required to offer every plan in every state, but all Medigap plans are required to offer the same basic benefits.

Medigap plans that cover the Part B deductible can no longer be sold to people who are newly eligible for Medicare on or after 01/01/2020. Those who already have Plan c and Plan f are grandfathered in.

In some states, some insurers offer a Medigap plan called Medicare SELECT. These plans generally have lower monthly premiums. Like some HMO plans, members must use in-network doctors and facilities, except in emergencies. Other than that, they function like a standard Medigap plan. (If you buy a Medicare SELECT plan, you have the right to change your mind within 12 months and switch to a standard Medigap plan.)

While federal law does not require insurance companies to sell Medigap plans to people under 65, in some states, there are state laws that require insurance companies to offer at least one kind of Medigap plan to people with Medicare under the age of 65. Some provide the right to buy a Medigap plan to ALL people under 65 who are eligible for Medicare; others only provide it for those under 65 who are eligible for Medicare because of a disability or ESRD. (Not all states offer a Medigap plan to those with ESRD.)

NOTE: Medicare Supplement Insurance cannot be used to help you pay for a Medicare Advantage Plan's out-of-pocket costs. In fact, it is illegal for anyone to sell you a Medigap plan if you're enrolled in a Medicare Advantage plan unless you are switching back to Original Medicare prior to your policy's effective date.

There are (10) standard Medigap plans.
(MA, MN, and WI have their own standard Medigap plans.)

MEDIGAP (2021)

PLAN a

Cost varies (by company and plan)

100% COVERAGE
- Part A coinsurance and hospital costs up to an additional 365 days after Medicare benefits are used up
- Part A hospice care coinsurance/copay
- Part B coinsurance/copay
- Blood (first 3 pints)

NO COVERAGE
- Part A deductible
- Part A skilled nursing (SNF) coinsurance
- Part B deductible
- Part B excess charge
- Foreign travel emergency care

ANNUAL OUT-OF-POCKET LIMIT: n/a

MEDIGAP (2021)

PLAN b

Cost varies (by company and plan)

100% COVERAGE
- Part A coinsurance and hospital costs up to an additional 365 days after Medicare benefits are used up
- Part A deductible
- Part A hospice care coinsurance/copay
- Part B coinsurance/copay
- Blood (first 3 pints)

NO COVERAGE
- Part A skilled nursing (SNF) coinsurance
- Part B deductible
- Part B excess charge
- Foreign travel emergency care

ANNUAL OUT-OF-POCKET LIMIT: n/a

MEDIGAP (2021)

PLAN C

Cost varies (by company and plan)

100% COVERAGE
- Part A coinsurance and hospital costs up to an additional 365 days after Medicare benefits are used up
- Part A deductible
- Part A hospice care coinsurance/copay
- Part A skilled nursing (SNF) coinsurance
- Part B coinsurance/copay
- Part B deductible
- Blood (first 3 pints)

No longer available to people who are "newly eligible" for Medicare as of 01/01/2020.

80% COVERAGE: Certain medically necessary emergency care is covered outside the U.S. if it begins during the first 60 days of your trip, and Medicare doesn't otherwise cover the care. (Foreign travel emergency coverage has a $250 annual deductible and a $50,000-lifetime limit.)

NO COVERAGE: Part B excess charge

ANNUAL OUT-OF-POCKET LIMIT: n/a

MEDIGAP (2021)

PLAN d

Cost varies (by company and plan)

100% COVERAGE
- Part A coinsurance and hospital costs up to an additional 365 days after Medicare benefits are used up
- Part A deductible
- Part A hospice care coinsurance/copay
- Part A skilled nursing (SNF) coinsurance
- Part B coinsurance/copay
- Blood (first 3 pints)

80% COVERAGE: Certain medically necessary emergency care is covered outside the U.S. if it begins during the first 60 days of your trip, and Medicare doesn't otherwise cover the care. (Foreign travel emergency coverage has a $250 annual deductible and a $50,000-lifetime limit.)

NO COVERAGE
- Part B deductible
- Part B excess charge

ANNUAL OUT-OF-POCKET LIMIT: n/a

MEDIGAP (2021)

PLAN f*

> **Cost varies** (by company and plan)

100% COVERAGE
- Part A coinsurance and hospital costs up to an additional 365 days after Medicare benefits are used up
- Part A deductible
- Part A hospice care coinsurance/copay
- Part A skilled nursing (SNF) coinsurance
- Part B coinsurance/copay
- Part B deductible
- Part B excess charge
- Blood (first 3 pints)

> **No longer available to people who are "newly eligible" for Medicare as of 01/01/2020.**

80% COVERAGE: Certain medically necessary emergency care is covered outside the U.S. if it begins during the first 60 days of your trip, and Medicare doesn't otherwise cover the care. (Foreign travel emergency coverage has a $250 annual deductible and a $50,000-lifetime limit.)

ANNUAL OUT-OF-POCKET LIMIT: n/a

*High-Deductible Plan f: You pay for all Medicare-covered costs up to $2,370 before your plan pays for anything. *(This is only available to those who were eligible for Medicare before1/1/2020.)*

MEDIGAP (2021)

PLAN g*

Cost varies (by company and plan)

100% COVERAGE
- Part A coinsurance and hospital costs up to an additional 365 days after Medicare benefits are used up
- Part A deductible
- Part A hospice care coinsurance/copay
- Part A skilled nursing (SNF) coinsurance
- Part B coinsurance/copay
- Part B excess charge
- Blood (first 3 pints)

80% COVERAGE: Certain medically necessary emergency care is covered outside the U.S. if it begins during the first 60 days of your trip, and Medicare doesn't otherwise cover the care. (Foreign travel emergency coverage has a $250 annual deductible and a $50,000-lifetime limit.)

NO COVERAGE: Part B deductible

ANNUAL OUT-OF-POCKET LIMIT: n/a

*High-Deductible Plan g: You pay for all Medicare-covered costs up to $2,370 before your plan pays for anything. *(This is only available to those who are newly eligible for Medicare on or after 1/1/2020.)*

MEDIGAP (2021)

PLAN k

Cost varies (by company and plan)

100% COVERAGE
- Part A coinsurance and hospital costs up to an additional 365 days after Medicare benefits are used up

50% COVERAGE
- Part A deductible
- Part A hospice care coinsurance/copay
- Part A skilled nursing (SNF) coinsurance
- Part B coinsurance/copay
- Blood (first 3 pints)

NO COVERAGE
- Part B deductible
- Part B excess charge
- Foreign travel emergency care

ANNUAL OUT-OF-POCKET LIMIT: $6,220
After you meet this limit and your annual Part B deductible, your Medigap plan pays 100%.

MEDIGAP (2021)

PLAN L

Cost varies (by company and plan)

100% COVERAGE
- Part A coinsurance and hospital costs up to an additional 365 days after Medicare benefits are used up

75% COVERAGE
- Part A deductible
- Part A hospice care coinsurance/copay
- Part A skilled nursing (SNF) coinsurance
- Part B coinsurance/copay
- Blood (first 3 pints)

NO COVERAGE
- Part B deductible
- Part B excess charge
- Foreign travel emergency care

ANNUAL OUT-OF-POCKET LIMIT: $3,110
After you meet this limit and your annual Part B deductible, your Medigap plan pays 100%.

MEDIGAP (2021)

PLAN m

Cost varies (by company and plan)

100% COVERAGE
- Part A coinsurance and hospital costs up to an additional 365 days after Medicare benefits are used up
- Part A hospice care coinsurance/copay
- Part A skilled nursing (SNF) coinsurance
- Part B coinsurance/copay
- Blood (first 3 pints)

80% COVERAGE: Certain medically necessary emergency care is covered outside the U.S. if it begins during the first 60 days of your trip, and Medicare doesn't otherwise cover the care. (Foreign travel emergency coverage has a $250 annual deductible and a $50,000-lifetime limit.)

50% COVERAGE: Part A deductible

NO COVERAGE
- Part B deductible
- Part B excess charge

ANNUAL OUT-OF-POCKET LIMIT: n/a

MEDIGAP (2021)

PLAN n

Cost varies (by company and plan)

100% COVERAGE
- Part A coinsurance and hospital costs up to an additional 365 days after Medicare benefits are used up
- Part A deductible
- Part A hospice care coinsurance/copay
- Part A skilled nursing (SNF) coinsurance
- Part B coinsurance/copay, except for a copay of up to $20 for some office visits and up to $50 for E.R. visits that don't result in inpatient admission
- Blood (first 3 pints)

80% COVERAGE: Certain medically necessary emergency care is covered outside the U.S. if it begins during the first 60 days of your trip, and Medicare doesn't otherwise cover the care. (Foreign travel emergency coverage has a $250 annual deductible and a $50,000-lifetime limit.)

NO COVERAGE
- Part B deductible
- Part B excess charge

ANNUAL OUT-OF-POCKET LIMIT: n/a

"Can I switch to another Medigap plan?"

Yes, but you'll most likely be required to go through medical underwriting *unless:*

1. You are still within your 6-month Medigap Open Enrollment Period, *or*
2. You have a special circumstance that qualifies you for a Special Enrollment Period, *or*
3. You have guaranteed issue rights, *or*
4. You live in a state that does not allow companies to use medical underwriting for Medigap.

If you want to stay with the same company but switch to a plan with less coverage and a lower premium: Your insurer *may* let you do this without going through medical underwriting. Ask your agent to assist you with this request.

If you want to switch to another company: Your agent can help you shop for a new policy and submit an application. When your policy arrives, you'll get a "30-day free look" period to decide whether or not you want to keep it.

NOTE: Ironically, you have to pay the premium on both policies during that one month "free look" period. If you return the new policy within 30 days you'll get a full refund of your premium.

MEDIGAP PLAN

a~n

MEDICARE SUPPLEMENT INSURANCE

YOUR COST FOR A MEDIGAP PLAN

Although all Medigap plans are standardized, your cost can vary greatly by company.

Are you comparing (red) apples to (red) apples?

When shopping for Medigap, it may be tempting to choose a policy based on its premium alone. But several other factors can influence how much you will pay for a Medigap policy over time. You must give this careful consideration before making a purchase.

Comparing two or more Medigap policies

Be sure to compare policies with the same plan letter, such as a **Medigap Plan g** policy to a **Medigap Plan g** policy.

Discounts

Some companies offer discounts to non-smokers, married people, households with a specified number of residents, and other criteria. Read the fine print carefully to see if the discount decreases over time. If so, your premiums will likely go up as you age even though the policy is not technically increasing due to you getting older.

History of rate increases

While this has no real bearing on what the insurance company will do with their premiums in the future, it's good to know what your experience would have been like if you had purchased a policy from this company a few years ago.

Rating (pricing) method

There are three different rating methods that an insurance company can use to set the price for a Medigap policy.

COMMUNITY-RATED POLICY: Everyone who purchases a community-rated policy pays the same premium, regardless of their age. Your premium will not increase due to you getting older but will likely increase due to inflation and other factors.

ISSUE-AGE-RATED POLICY: Your premium is based on your age at the time of purchase. (When the policy is "issued" to you.) Your premium will not increase due to you getting older but will likely increase due to inflation and other factors.

ATTAINED-AGE-RATED POLICY: Your premium is based on your current age. (The age you have "attained.") Therefore, it will increase due to you getting older and will likely increase due to inflation and other factors, as well.

Financial rating

A carrier with a B+ or higher rating will typically be more established and have more financial stability.

MEDIGAP ENROLLMENT PERIODS

Those who are 65 years of age or older and enrolled in Medicare Part B may apply for a Medigap plan at any time of the year. The best time to enroll is during your Medigap Open Enrollment Period.

Medigap Open Enrollment Period (OEP)

This 6-month period begins the first day of the month in which you are 65 years of age or older and you have Part B. During this time you have **guaranteed issue rights.** This means that you can buy any Medigap plan the company sells in your market for the same price as someone of the same age who has no pre-existing health conditions; your application cannot be declined.

If you miss the Medigap Open Enrollment Period and do not qualify for a Special Enrollment Period, most insurers will require you to go through medical underwriting to determine your insurability (unless your state allows special exceptions). If you have a pre-existing condition, the insurance company can:

- Decline your application.
- Accept your application but restrict your coverage with a 6-month "pre-existing condition waiting period." During this time, your pre-existing condition will only be covered by Medicare; you will have to pay the full coinsurance/copayment amount.
- Charge you a higher premium.

If you have a chronic or critical illness and want to purchase a Medigap plan, it's important to use this enrollment period (or a Special Enrollment Period, if you qualify) to ensure that you are guaranteed coverage at no additional cost and with no waiting period.

Special Circumstances | Special Enrollment Periods (SEP)

If you are 65 years of age or older, and certain life events happen after your 6-month Medigap Open Enrollment Period has passed, you may be able to qualify for a guaranteed-issue Medigap plan if you apply within 63 days of (when):

- Through no fault of your own, you lose an employer-sponsored insurance plan that supplemented your Medicare. This Special Enrollment Period begins 60 days before your current plan expires, *or*
- You move out of the area that's covered by a Medigap plan, *or*
- Your insurer goes bankrupt or misrepresents a provision in your plan, *or*
- You disenroll from a Medicare Advantage plan (that you had enrolled in when you first became eligible for Medicare) within 12 months of enrolling in it.

Some states have additional Medigap rules:

- **CALIFORNIA:** Anyone who is enrolled in a Medigap plan can use the "California Birthday Rule" to change to any other Medigap plan with equal or lesser benefits offered by any company, with guaranteed issue rights. You have 60 days starting on your birthday to make the switch.
- **CONNECTICUT:** All Medigap plans are community rated and you have guaranteed issue rights. If you have a pre-existing health condition, or you've had no prior creditable

coverage (or a gap in coverage), you may have a waiting period of up to six months.

- **MAINE:** Each year, each insurer must designate a one-month guaranteed issue period when any applicant will be accepted in **Medigap Plan a.** Insurers must also offer you a guaranteed issue plan if you apply for a Medigap plan within 90 days of losing coverage from an individual health insurance plan, a group health plan through your employer, or MaineCare. (Some restrictions apply.) And anyone with a Medigap plan who has never had a gap in coverage (that supplements Medicare) of more than 90 days since your Open Enrollment period can switch to a plan with equal or lesser benefits from any insurer at any time of the year with guaranteed issue.

- **MISSOURI:** Anyone with a Medigap plan can change to another Medigap plan with guaranteed issue. You have from 30 days before your policy's annual anniversary date until 30 days after it to make the switch.

- **NEW YORK:** All Medigap plans are guaranteed issue, but if you have a pre-existing condition, you may have a waiting period of up to six months. Medigap insurers are required to reduce the waiting period by the number of days that you were covered under some form of "creditable" coverage so long as there were no breaks in coverage of more than 63 calendar days.

- **OREGON:** Anyone who is enrolled in a Medigap plan can use the "Birthday Rule" to switch to any other Medigap plan with equal or lesser benefits that are offered by any company during their birth month with a guaranteed issue. This enrollment period starts on your birthday and ends 30 days later.

OTHER MEDICARE HEALTH PLANS

Medicare Cost plans

These plans are only available in certain areas of the country. In some ways, they are similar to a Medicare Advantage plan and in other ways, they are very different. For example:

- You can enroll in a Medicare Cost plan even if you only have Part B.
- You can join any time the plan is accepting new members.
- You can leave the plan at any time and return to Original Medicare.
- You have the option of going to in-network or out-of-network providers. When you go out-of-network your services are covered by Original Medicare and you pay the Part A & Part B deductibles and coinsurance.
- If the plan includes prescription drug coverage, you can choose to get your prescriptions from the plan *or* enroll in a Medicare Prescription Drug plan.

Another type of Medicare Cost plan only provides coverage for Part B services, and never includes Part D. (Part A services are covered through Original Medicare.) These plans are either sponsored by employer or union group health plans or offered by companies that don't provide Part A services.

Programs of All-Inclusive Care for the Elderly

PACE is a Medicare/Medicaid program that helps people who need a nursing home level of care to get the health care services they need in their community, such as in their own home or at a PACE center, so they don't have to be confined to a nursing home or other care facility.

Those who are enrolled in PACE have a team of health care professionals who take the time to get to know you and work closely with you and your family to make sure you are getting the level of coordinated care and services you need.

To be eligible for coverage, you must be:
- 55 years of age, or older
- Certified by your state as needing a nursing home level of care
- Able to live safely in the community with the help of PACE services (at the time of enrollment)
- Living in the service area of a PACE organization

If you have Medicare and Medicaid, there's no monthly premium for the long-term care portion of your PACE benefit. If you have Medicare only, you will be charged a monthly premium to cover the long-term care portion of your PACE benefits plus a premium for Medicare Part D prescription drugs. There is no deductible or copayment for any service, care, or drug approved by your health care team.

Medicare Demonstrations/Pilot Programs

Medicare periodically conducts research studies to test improvements in their coverage, payment, and quality of care. These special projects usually run for a limited time, in specific areas, for a specific group of people. Call 1-800-MEDICARE to get more information on these programs.

WHICH MEDICARE PLAN IS BEST FOR ME?

Let's review your options.

If you have Original Medicare (Part A & Part B) only:

- You can go to any hospital, doctor, or provider in the U.S. that accepts Medicare.
- Part A covers your inpatient hospital stay, skilled nursing care in a skilled nursing facility, home health care, and hospice care services. Your out-of-pocket costs include a monthly premium ($0/month for most people), hospital deductible, hospital coinsurance, and skilled nursing facility coinsurance.
- Part B covers your medically necessary services, mental health care, preventative and screening services, and durable medical equipment. Your out-of-pocket costs include a monthly premium, annual deductible, medical copayment, and medical coinsurance.
- You have NO coverage for outpatient prescription drugs, routine dental care (cleanings, exams, X-rays, or dentures), routine vision care (exams for glasses/contact lenses), routine hearing care (exams for hearing aids), routine foot care, or routine preventative physical exams.
- There is NO LIMIT on your Part A & Part B out-of-pocket costs, which can potentially add up to a financially catastrophic amount of money.

Medicare plans are also available through private companies to help you fill some of the gaps in coverage and provide financial protection. The option that's best for you may be very different from the option that's best for your spouse or friends because we all have different needs, personal preferences, and priorities. There are three ways to fill the gaps in coverage and minimize your financial risk:

OPTION 1:

Enroll in a Medicare Advantage plan (Part C) with prescription drug coverage. This option provides all your Medicare Part A & Part B benefits, fills the drug coverage gap, and (usually) gives you some extra coverage, such as routine dental, vision, and hearing care, and more. And all plans have a maximum out-of-pocket limit to provide you with a financial safety net. Most plans have a network of providers. (PPO's will generally allow you to go out-of-network to any doctor or facility that accepts Medicare, at a higher cost.)

OPTION 2:

Stay in Original Medicare (Part A & Part B) and add Part D. This option fills the drug coverage gap, but there's NO LIMIT on how much your Part A & Part B out-of-pocket costs can add up to. You have no financial safety net unless you receive financial assistance from the government, such as through Medicaid or a Medicare savings program. You can go to any doctor or facility in the U.S. that accepts Medicare.

OPTION 3:

Stay in Original Medicare (Part A & Part B) and add Part D plus a Medigap Plan to your coverage. This option fills the drug coverage gap and provides you with a financial safety net by helping you cover some of your Part A & Part B out-of-pocket costs. You can go to any doctor or facility that accepts Medicare.

Here's another way to visualize this:

3 Ways to Fill the Gaps and Minimize Your Financial Risk

Enroll in a Medicare Advantage plan
with prescription drug coverage.

Stay in Original Medicare +
enroll in a Medicare Prescription Drug plan.

Stay in Original Medicare +
enroll in a Medicare Prescription Drug plan +
buy a Medicare Supplement Insurance (Medigap) plan

Now it's time to meet with an agent.

Working with an agent who is familiar with the Medicare plans in your market will save you an enormous amount of time and frustration!

NOTE: An agent who works for an insurance company is called a "captive" agent. (Captive agents can only sell policies offered by their employer.) A broker is an independent agent who works for you. (Brokers can sell policies offered by many different companies.)

A good agent:

- Asks if you understand what Medicare covers and doesn't cover *before* launching into a sales presentation. If you don't understand something, they will take the time to explain it to you and answer all of your questions.
- Does a quick, but thorough needs analysis to evaluate your needs, personal preferences, and priorities.
- Educates you about the differences between a Medicare Advantage plan and a Medigap plan, and has *you* decide which type of coverage *you* would like to have. (It's not about which type of coverage *they'd* like you to have.)
- Gives you options.
- Reaches out to you during the Annual Enrollment Period to help you review the upcoming changes to your plan to make sure that it still fits your needs well for the coming year.
- Helps you resolve issues if they arise.
- Returns your phone calls in a timely manner.
- Is a trusted advisor that you can rely on, like a true friend.

FINANCIAL ASSISTANCE PROGRAMS

Financial assistance programs are available for those who meet certain income and resource limits. These can help you pay for some or all of your Medicare out-of-pocket costs.

Extra Help

This Medicare low-income subsidy (LIS) program may help pay for your prescription drugs.

Medicaid

This joint federal and state program helps some people with limited income and resources with their medical costs. Medicaid offers benefits that are not normally covered by Medicare, like nursing home care and personal care services.

Medicare Savings Programs

This state program may help people with limited income and resources pay for their out-of-pocket costs.

- **Qualified Medicare Beneficiary (QMB)**
  Helps pay for Part A & Part B premiums, deductibles, copayments, and coinsurance.
- **Specified Low-Income Medicare Beneficiary (SLMB)**
  Helps pay for Part B premiums only.
- **Qualifying Individual (QI)**
  Helps pay for Part B premiums only. Funding is limited; applications are granted on a first-come, first-served basis.
- **Qualified Disabled & Working Individual (QDWI)**
  Helps pay for Part A premiums only.

NOTE: Those who qualify for QMB, SLMB, or QI automatically qualify for Extra Help.

Programs for people in U.S. territories

Financial assistance is available in Puerto Rico, U.S. Virgin Islands, Guam, Northern Mariana Islands, and American Samoa for those who need help paying for Medicare costs.

State Pharmaceutical Assistance Programs

Your state may offer a program such as Senior Rx/Disability Rx to help you pay for prescription drugs.

Supplemental Social Security Income

This program pays benefits to disabled adults (and children) who have little or no income and provides cash to meet basic needs for food, clothing, and shelter. It also pays benefits to people 65 and older without disabilities who meet the financial limits.

TRAVELING WITH MEDICARE INSURANCE

"Am I covered by Medicare when I travel?"

That depends. Where are you going? And which Medicare plan do you have?

For example, if you're on a cruise ship and you have Original Medicare (Part A & Part B) only, you may only be covered while the ship is in U.S. waters or, in some cases, within the territorial waters adjoining the land areas of the U.S. Once that ship is six hours away from the nearest U.S. port, you are basically in whatever country the ship is registered in. If a foreign flag is flying on the mainmast and you have Original Medicare, your insurance may offer little or no protection or reimbursement for the costs of any medical treatments received on board that ship. Whereas, if you have a Medicare Advantage plan or Medigap plan that provides emergency and urgently needed medical care globally, you may be fine.

Traveling with Original Medicare (only)

If you get hurt or sick while traveling within the 50 states, the District of Columbia, Puerto Rico, U.S. Virgin Islands, Guam, Northern Mariana Islands, or American Samoa, you can go to ANY doctor, hospital, or other facilities that accept Medicare. However, Medicare generally does NOT cover your health care when you travel outside the U.S. and its territories, except in rare circumstances, such as if:

- You're in the U.S. when a medical emergency happens and a hospital in a foreign country is closer than the hospital that can treat your injuries.
- You have a medical emergency while traveling by the most direct route from Alaska to another state, you can be treated in a Canadian hospital if it's closer than the nearest U.S. hospital.
- You live in the U.S. and a foreign hospital is closer to your home than the nearest U.S. hospital that can treat you, you can go to the foreign hospital, whether you have an emergency or not.

Traveling with a Medigap plan

Medigap plans simply help you pay for your Part A & Part B out-of-pocket costs, so as long as you're covered by Original Medicare, you're good to go. If you have a Medigap plan **c, d, f, g, m,** or **n,** you are covered for foreign travel emergency care, as well.

Traveling with a Medicare Advantage plan

You are covered for emergency and urgently needed medical care everywhere in the United States and its territories. Some plans provide global coverage, as well. If yours does and you receive medical care abroad, be sure to get an itemized copy of the bill in English.

NOTE: Most Medicare Advantage plans will disenroll you and place you back in Original Medicare if you travel outside of your service area continuously for more than 6 months.

If you are planning to be away from home for an extended period of time, talk to your agent about your options for coverage. Some Medicare Advantage plans have a "traveler's" benefit that will allow you to be away from home for up to 12 months at a time and will give you access to a network of providers in other states.

Your agent will be happy to help you find a plan that fits your needs!

ABOUT
THE AUTHOR

Linda A. Bell is an independent insurance broker and the founder of the **Medicare Insurance *Simplified* Toolbox**™ for agents. Included in this bundle is a detailed Needs Analysis worksheet, a personalized "Medicare Insurance *Simplified* Overview" presentation, and a personalized edition of this ebook, plus lots of tips and step-by-step tutorials to help

agents work in the field with confidence and ease!

"This is the fastest, easiest way to educate people about Medicare — and grow your referral-based business!"

To learn more about Linda, visit: HeartToHeartInsurance.com. See: (blog post) "How I Got From Way Over There To Medicare."

A note from the author:

I welcome your questions, comments, and testimonials! Please send them to Linda@HeartToHeartInsurance.com.

From the heart,
Linda A. Bell

Made in the USA
Middletown, DE
30 November 2021

53854831R00058